1,000,000 Books

are available to read at

Forgotten Books

www.ForgottenBooks.com

Read online
Download PDF
Purchase in print

ISBN 978-1-331-36468-9
PIBN 10179819

This book is a reproduction of an important historical work. Forgotten Books uses state-of-the-art technology to digitally reconstruct the work, preserving the original format whilst repairing imperfections present in the aged copy. In rare cases, an imperfection in the original, such as a blemish or missing page, may be replicated in our edition. We do, however, repair the vast majority of imperfections successfully; any imperfections that remain are intentionally left to preserve the state of such historical works.

Forgotten Books is a registered trademark of FB &c Ltd.
Copyright © 2018 FB &c Ltd.
FB &c Ltd, Dalton House, 60 Windsor Avenue, London, SW19 2RR.
Company number 08720141. Registered in England and Wales.

For support please visit www.forgottenbooks.com

1 MONTH OF FREE READING

at

www.ForgottenBooks.com

By purchasing this book you are eligible for one month membership to ForgottenBooks.com, giving you unlimited access to our entire collection of over 1,000,000 titles via our web site and mobile apps.

To claim your free month visit: www.forgottenbooks.com/free179819

* Offer is valid for 45 days from date of purchase. Terms and conditions apply.

English
Français
Deutsche
Italiano
Español
Português

www.forgottenbooks.com

Mythology Photography **Fiction**
Fishing Christianity **Art** Cooking
Essays Buddhism Freemasonry
Medicine **Biology** Music **Ancient Egypt** Evolution Carpentry Physics
Dance Geology **Mathematics** Fitness
Shakespeare **Folklore** Yoga Marketing
Confidence Immortality Biographies
Poetry **Psychology** Witchcraft
Electronics Chemistry History **Law**
Accounting **Philosophy** Anthropology
Alchemy Drama Quantum Mechanics
Atheism Sexual Health **Ancient History**
Entrepreneurship Languages Sport
Paleontology Needlework Islam
Metaphysics Investment Archaeology
Parenting Statistics Criminology
Motivational

OF

DARTMOUTH COLLEGE:

BEING

Historical Collections and Personal Reminiscences.

BY NATHAN CROSBY,

OF THE CLASS OF 1820.

READ BEFORE THE ALUMNI AT THE
COMMENCEMENT IN 1875.

PUBLISHED BY REQUEST AND ORDER OF THE ALUMNI.

HANOVER:
J. B. PARKER.
1876.

LD
1438
C8

PRINTED BY THE REPUBLICAN PRESS ASSOCIATION, CONCORD, N. H.

Gentlemen, Alumni of Dartmouth College:

INTRODUCTION.

I do not regard this as a lecture, or history of the college, but simply historical data which I have gathered in my reading, and my own personal reminiscences of the origin and life of the college to the end of the first *fifty* years of its existence. The college charter was obtained in 1769. Six years ago we celebrated its first centennial. I am of the class of 1820, just midway its first one hundred years. I had personal acquaintance with the second President Wheelock, and met Mr. Gray, who visited the college in 1827. Both were graduates in the first class in 1771. I lived at one time near Rev. Mr. Miltimore, of Newbury, Mass., of the class of 1774, and was familiarly acquainted with Nathaniel Adams, Esquire, of the class of 1775, who was the author of the "Portsmouth Annals," and one of the founders of the New Hampshire Historical Society in 1823. Caleb Bingham, of the class of 1782, furnished my boyhood's satchel with his "Young Ladies' Accidence," "American Preceptor," and "Columbian Orator," and Daniel Adams, of the class of 1797, with his "Scholars' Arithmetic, or Federal Accountant." When I came to the study of Latin, I was introduced to the Latin Grammar of John Smith, A. M., of the class of 1773, and a professor of the college. When I entered in 1816, I found, as members of the faculty, Prof. Ebenezer Adams, of the class of 1791, and Prof. Roswell Shurtleff, class of 1799, with President Francis Brown, of the class of 1805. My childhood's pastor was Rev. Samuel Hidden, of the class of 1781, and the first lawyer I ever saw was James Otis Freeman, of the class of 1797. In fact, as I look over the catalogue, I find personal acquaintances in almost all the classes of the first fifty years. My college life covered the period of the great legal controversy between the "University" and the "College," or, perhaps, rather, between the state and the college; and I have thought it well to give the Alumni the history of certain academical events of that period, lest evidence of them shall soon fail to exist.

The saying that "the world moves on," was never more impressively proven than in the history of Dartmouth college. We are here to-day, joyous in our goodly heritage. We take pride and pleasure in our distinguished faculty; in these college buildings; in this same old common; in the same old hills, river, and skies, with buoyant hope and expectation of future enlargement and glory; its days of poverty and struggles for life all past; its scant accommodations changed to elegant buildings, dormitories, observatory, library, and gymnasium; several department schools; large funds for scholarships, and donations changed in amount from a few days' labor in 1770, to half a million dollars in 1875.* But this manhood had a wondrous birth and infancy,—an infancy fed from the paps of faith and prayer, and upheld by a Power stronger than fire, floods, or winter's frosts.

CHARTER.

The charter of Dartmouth college was granted by His Majesty King George the Third, at the solicitation of Gov.

---

* Hon. Tappan Wentworth, of Lowell, Mass., who died June 12, last, gave by will his whole estate to the college, subject to a few legacies and annuities, and to its accumulation to half a million before application to uses of the college. The property consists mostly of real estate of great present as well as prospective value, in the business centre of the city. It has been valued by appraisers at nearly $300,000, having an income last year of about $20,000 Mr. Wentworth was born in Dover, N. H., and belonged to the Wentworth family, of which Gov. John Wentworth, who granted the charter, was also a member, both uniting in William Wentworth, the emigrant to America, whose descent is traced, through a distinguished line of Wentworths, to Rynold, in 1066 He was an eminent counsellor at law, and ex-member of congress. He received the honorary degree of Master of Arts here in 1850, where three of the Wentworth family have also received the degree of Doctor of Laws, Hon John Wentworth, of Chicago, ex-member of congress, being one. Having lost his only child, a delightful son, twelve years old, twenty years ago, his love of learning, attachment to his native state, and pride in his eminent kindred who administered the government of the state in its early history for forty-six years, undoubtedly moved him to this great endowment—his "life work," as he said to a friend.

John Wentworth, royal governor of New Hampshire, December 13, 1769, who was moved thereto by Rev. Eleazer Wheelock, of Lebanon, Connecticut. Dr. Wheelock asked a charter for "Dartmouth *Academy*," but obtained a charter for "Dartmouth *College*." He had prepared his charter, and suggested trustees, but the governor changed the terms of it, and also the managing power. We cannot suppose these changes were made without courteous suggestion on the one part, and proper submission on the other. Governor Wentworth, who was a man of education and travel abroad, grasped fully Dr. Wheelock's views and labors, in the united forces of religion and education, to civilize the Indian as well as to elevate their own countrymen. Dr. Wheelock had a great plan for the enlargement of the borders of Zion, and the governor desired to turn it to the benefit of the people, and the honor of his administration. The charter was arranged, the trustees named, and the college established. The governor and four provincial officers were made trustees by the charter. Dr. Wheelock and six of his friends, mostly Connecticut clergymen, completed the board. Not a clergyman of New Hampshire was upon it.

CLERGYMEN THE TEACHERS OF THE TIME.

When this charter was granted there was only one *academy* (Byfield) in all New England, except perhaps the institution at Warren, R. I.,—which was afterwards removed to Providence and became a college,—and only two colleges, Harvard and Yale. From the settlement of the country, teachers of schools, and young men intending to go to college, were almost wholly instructed and prepared by clergymen. The ministers of that day were generally graduates, and some of them became distinguished teachers. Dr. Wheelock had been a most successful preacher in many parts of New England during the Great Awakening of 1740,—a preacher after Jonathan Edwards's own heart. He had become so universally known as a man of great power as well as of great piety, that he had no difficulty in obtaining students when he opened his house as a teacher.

Many of the clergymen of Dr. Wheelock's time were men of extraordinary culture and power. They came forth from and had been trained in a long line of men of Puritan thought and opinion. They had devoted themselves to the two great twin doctrines, of freedom in faith and in government. The earliest ministers among the Pilgrim and Puritan emigrants had been driven from their native lands because they had made themselves obnoxious to both church and state by their independent and persistent discussion of the great gospel inherent right of man to believe for himself and to govern himself. They were men of learning, men of enthusiasm and courage, and fled hither, bearing the precious seed of their new and better way to rule and to live to this new and virgin soil, where time and space and a growing people would give them a home and a hearing. These men at once, as the first living breath of freedom, established schools along-side the pulpit, as the key-stone of the arch upon which their new temple of freedom could rest and abide. They prepared teachers for the schools, fitted young men for college, became professors and lecturers, and gave sentiment and tone to public opinion and thought in sermons, addresses, pamphlet discussions, and wide-spread correspondence. They visited the schools, catechised the children, and expounded the new gospel of freedom to the people, as next in importance to the gospel of grace—a gospel which gave "God his due, and Cæsar his, and the people theirs." Having never been allowed to hold civil office or vote in the old country, they abstained from both for many years in the early history of the colonies. The future historian of our colonial life will find facts and influence enough to award to the clergymen, before the revolution, the maximum share in originating, building up, and sustaining the public sentiment and courage which accomplished our independence.

The same wonderful talent, learning, and consecration of the early clergy to the cause and growth of learning, religion, and freedom, continued down to the early years of the present century. Clergymen were as distinct from the people then, as Catholic priests are now from their adherents. There were half a dozen of such old clergymen in my neighborhood in my young years. They were grave men, in long coats and vests and small-clothes, with knee- and shoe-buckles, with the tricornered or cocked-up hat, as it was called. They rode through the towns on horseback, carrying in one hand a long cane as a badge of office, and a reminder to Rosinante to be quiet at times as well as grave always. The children knew them, thought of their catechism, and gave them a wide berth—stood still and straight as soldiers, made obeisance, and stared them out of sight.

DR. WHEELOCK AND THE GREAT AWAKENING.

Dr. Wheelock was the great grandson of Rev. Ralph Wheelock, of Shropshire, who was one of those eminent non-conformist preachers, and, suffering persecution for dissenting from the established religion, came to New England in 1637, and settled in Dedham, Mass. The Doctor was the only son of Ralph and Ruth (Huntington) Wheelock, and was born in Windham, Conn., in May, 1711, was graduated at Yale in 1733, and was ordained and settled over the North Society in Lebanon, Conn., in 1735. His earnest and eloquent labors soon aroused great religious interest among his people. The "Great Awakening of 1740," as it is now historically called, soon followed, and the whole country became absorbed in the most wonderful religious excitement, perhaps phrensy, known in our history or the history of the church. Dr. Wheelock took a place in the very front rank of the preachers and agitators of this religious earthquake. He was a live man from the commencement of his ministry. He had heard the thunderings of Whitefield, and the mighty reasonings of Edwards at Northampton upon *justification by faith and not by works*—a living faith, and not dead works. Ministers had been settled by towns over parishes for life, and the churches were sunk in a lifeless orthodoxy. Pastors and peoples found themselves unequally yoked. Great minds became inactive for want of appreciative hearers; and, again, cultivated congregations starved for mental food. Dull formality and spiritual pride were fast removing the Puritan landmark of salvation by faith in the Son of God. The half-way covenant by baptism was taking the place of the new birth as a qualification for church membership, and, if a baptized person was refused the communion, although leading an irreligious life, the refusing watchful pastor was open to prosecution for damages in a civil suit. Spiritual death and desolation were fast darkening the fair fields of Puritan labor and expectation. All the churches were now shaken up by the great question of a new birth, and whether such "new lights" as Whitefield, Wheelock, Pomroy, and others should be suffered to preach in churches or to congregations not their own, causing general disquiet among pastors and their people. Many ministers, and some of the people in most parishes, objected. Pulpits were refused them, and suits were brought against them for preaching without permission in parishes not their own, and also for refusing to admit to the communion persons of irreligious life when baptized. But the work went on, multitudes were born into the kingdom, and a clearer line between the righteous and the wicked on earth was drawn and scripturally maintained; and although many good men long doubted the purity of intention and the legitimate success of the *Awakeners* as ambassadors of Heaven, the history of the church before and since the Great Awakening will compel the record of that mysterious yet fruitful period as a new departure in the life, purity, and power of the church. A recovery of lost vitality, and the introduction of a higher Christian life, bear date from that spiritual upheaving. It was like the great revival by Peter and John at the Pentecost, in the Sandwich Islands a few years ago, and now late in England and Scotland under Moody and Sankey.

Dr. Wheelock was eloquent and attractive, energetic, fearless, and laborious. He travelled from town to town, and preached two or three sermons almost daily. His journal from Oct. 19 to Nov. 16, 1741, shows him in twenty towns, and that he preached forty sermons, besides his "conferences," "counsels," &c. It is said he preached in one year one hundred more sermons than there were days in the year.*

Dr. Trumbull says,—"He was a gentleman of comely figure, of a mild, winning aspect; his voice smooth and harmonious— the best, by far, that I ever heard. He had the entire com-

---

* See *Am. Qr. Register*, August, 1837.

mand of it. His gesture was natural, but not redundant. His preaching and addresses were close and pungent, and yet winning beyond almost all comparison, so that his audience would be melted even into tears before they were aware of it."

I have thus introduced to your consideration the character of the early ministers of the country, and the Great Awakening, that you might gain a proper knowledge and appreciation of the distinguished founder of our college. The intolerance which drove his great-grandfather from Shropshire gave character and tenacity to his love of freedom. His love and zeal for Christ and his cause gave him pilgrim self-denial and power. His first great work, as an *itinerant preacher*, raised him to the high position of yoke-fellow of Whitefield in the Great Awakening, and shadowed forth his great good will to man, however and wherever his Lord and Master might call him.

BETTER FACILITIES FOR EDUCATION CALLED FOR.

The awakening sifted the ministry, caused marked denominational lines, and stimulated the Puritan element to new securities as well as enlargement. The population of all New England amounted then to about 700,000; the distant forests were being subdued by a prosperous, hardy people, and the early settlements were calling for more culture and social pleasures. Clergymen were more than ever stimulated to educate the people to the plane of ability to judge safely the great questions in theology, as well as politics, involved in the discussions and decisions of those experimental days. Dr. Wheelock lost no time in marking out his work. He quieted himself down to the ordinary duties of a pastor again. But his parish was small, and his people would only about half pay his little salary;* so, minister-like, he opened his house for a school, and had no lack of pupils.

---

* Rev Hugh Adams, of Durham, N H., who continued there in the ministry from 1718 to 1750, petitioned the Provincial Assembly in 1738, that "a neglect to pay a minister may be made penal, and presentable by the grand jury, as it was in Massachusetts, which he considered the principal reason why the people of that province had been proportionably spared from the throat pestilence, and other impoverishing, more than New Hampshire "
—*N. H. Hist. Col.*, 239.

EDUCATIONAL POVERTY.

It is well to look for a moment at the educational opportunities in the country at the commencement of Dr. Wheelock's school. Not an academy, not a medical school for fifty years after, a law college or theological seminary for seventy years. Young men could reach a preparation for professional life only by overcoming the greatest discouragements. The clergymen were generally graduates, and were the teachers of the young men and women of their various parishes, so as to fit them to become teachers of the common schools. Some clergymen kept their classics bright, and fitted the young men for college, while others became distinguished as theologians, and attracted the graduates for preparation for the ministry. Dr. Woods, of Boscawen, partially or wholly fitted a hundred young men for college, Daniel and Ezekiel Webster, *par nobile fratrum*,—a brace of eminent pupils,—being of the number. Dr. Spring of Newburyport, Edwards of Northampton, and Emmons of Franklin, made academies after the Roman and Greek pattern, and Dr. Burton, in the quiet little town of Thetford, Vt., sent out over sixty ministers, many of them rising to eminent standing in theology. Rev. Thomas Parker, a learned divine, instructed ten to fifteen yearly for the pulpit, within fifty years after the arrival of the Mayflower.

INDIAN CIVILIZATION.

In December, 1743, Samson Occom, a Mohegan Indian, nineteen years old, came along and knocked at the Doctor's school for admission. The good Doctor received him, and kept him in his family, and educated him four or five years. Occom was quick to learn, ready to receive the benefit of civilized culture, and became "a preacher of distinction." Dr. Wheelock now formed his new and great idea of Christianizing the Indians by educating them with white men, who would return with them to the forests as missionaries.

There had prevailed from the early settlement of the country the sentiment that the emigrants must Christianize these heathen Indians, not only because they ought to be Christianized, but because the emigrants were taking their lands by purchase or power, and driving them farther back into the wilderness. So fixed was this sentiment in the hearts of the King and the agents of the grantees of lands in the new world, and the people here, that recognition of the obligation and covenant of effort to that end were incorporated into royal grants, and even into the charter of the college in 1769.

MOOR'S CHARITY SCHOOL.

Dr. Wheelock's new idea of a better way to convert the Indians filled his soul like the "Great Awakening." It was another field of religious effort, equal to his great capacities. He called in young Indian men and women from various tribes to his school, and put his young missionary students to instruct them and meliorate their manners and habits, to *unforest* them. He appealed to the benevolent to aid him in support of the school. His pulpit power and persuasion, his faith and zeal, gave life and direction to the great sentiment at home and abroad, that for his lands the Indians must have the gospel, and that his new plan would accomplish the great end. He had solicited certain clergymen to stand as trustees, says President Styles, in his diary. Public sentiment widened and increased as his pupils and missionaries multiplied. The combined missionary power of the white and red man seemed full of promise, and gave strength to Christian faith and zeal. Occom was sent to England and Scotland in 1762, as a specimen minister of his Indian school, to preach the same gospel, to show its power upon the wild men of the forest,* and to pray for aid in the great work. Occom was received with great enthusiasm by the nobility, clergymen, and people, and returned with nearly 12,000 pounds, from his collections abroad. Joshua Moor, a neighbor and friend of Dr. Wheelock, had given a house and a few acres of land for his school, which had taken the name of "Moor's Charity School." The legislatures of Connecticut, Massachusetts, and New Hampshire granted aid, and he received cordial and flattering approbation of the leading clergymen in Connecticut and other states, half a dozen

---

" As an exhibition to the people of England of what Christianity would do for the nations of North America." DeForest's Hist. of Ind. of Conn., 458.

governors, various judges of courts, lawyers, merchants, and men in high governmental positions.* The Doctor had missionaries out among the tribes, who sent in pupils, so that his numbers increased to twenty-five, and his Indian schoolmasters at work in wigwams counted more than half a dozen.

The second decade of promised success, however, developed more than one worm at the root. It began to appear that the Indian graduates were not more than half converted; that a return to the woods revived too readily their love of hunting and fishing, the chase and sports of Indian life, the vagrancy and cruelties of old habits and old grudges. The political difficulties between the colonies and the mother country, between the royal governors and the people, had become serious, and the tribes were taking sides with the King against the colonies, and they now became suspicious of the new interest manifested in them, and doubted Christian love and men. It was apparent, moreover, that the Indian pupil was impatient of the restraints of civilized life and cultivated society, and hungered for the wild viands and free air of his tribe—very ominous facts.

FEARS OF FAILURE.

Dr. Wheelock seemed now to fear that the second great effort of his life might come to an inglorious end; that his great idea of union and harmony in the education of English and Indian missionaries and schoolmasters might ere long fail of promised and anticipated accomplishment, and that the donors and sympathizers might hold him in derision. They had considered the plan, and approved; had given sympathy, prayers, and funds; and were looking with great interest for much of the success which the Doctor's enthusiastic letters and "Narratives" led them to expect,—while he had reasonable forebodings that Indian infirmities, prejudices, customs, and indolence, as well as their probable position of enemies in the threatening strife for independence of the colonies, *matters wholly beyond his control*, would ere long bring an end to his school as an exploded idea. He therefore devised and deter-

---

* See historical papers, &c., in "The 150th Anniversary of the Organization of the Church in Columbia, Conn., Oct., 1866" (Dr. Wheelock's church), for list of names.

mined on a new departure, a new and more hopeful effort. We now come to the third and last great effort of his life.

NEW DEPARTURE.

Dr. Wheelock had now been a pastor in Lebanon twenty-five years. The men about him were eminent in politics, in theology, and in general literature and the sciences. No town in Connecticut, or elsewhere even, could boast of having produced so many great and good men during that century as this same Lebanon. Among them was our distinguished Jeremiah Mason, one of the learned and eloquent advocates for the college in the great lawsuit. He was born in Lebanon during Dr. Wheelock's pastorate, and may have been baptized by him—a man of more legal knowledge and power than any other this side of Chief Justice Marshall. And Dr. Wheelock was the eminent man among these Lebanon men, and must not fail in judgment or executive power. His first great idea for Indian conversion must not fail. He must move his school and quit his pastorate. He astonished himself by his resolution, and the world by his purpose, to remove his school into the wilderness. He must take his wife from friends of culture and refinement, and his sons and daughters, growing up to maturity, from polished circles of friendship, to the rough life of frontiersmen.

"How can I leave thee, Paradise?" he might well have exclaimed. "And how can I see my plan, the great idea of my life, and the labor of my best years, come to naught?" he did ask himself. "This school must not fail to accomplish its work. These funds must not be wasted or returned. By the help of God, this will I do: I will take it into the woods.* I will let the young men of the forest bring their bow and gun and fishing-rod, that they may indulge in their native sports. Maybe the transition from the woods to open fields, from their *huts* to our *dwellings*, from skins and blankets to our careful costumes, from their wild life to our

---

* "A better place for an Indian seminary than the more thickly settled colony of Connecticut"—(*De Fore*st),—although there were then over thirteen hundred Indians in Conn. The new idea seemed to be an endeavor to reach the distant tribes.

cultivated habits, is too great a trial of their independence and patience. I will train, also, in their company, and along with them, young men from among us who desire to get an education, and become missionaries among the Indians. They will assimilate in thought and habits, and the Indian shall take back to the forest a yoke-fellow in the great work of education and evangelization."

Dr. Wheelock now announced to his church and the world, as early as 1767, that he should take his school and remove to a place nearer the Indians, and should unite with it the functions of an academy. A strange idea—an unheard-of thought—supremely ridiculous! An academy in the woods, remote from population on one side, and with a forest upon the other! Harvard college in Massachusetts, and Yale in Connecticut, had both been located with close access to the large towns on a long line of coast, and were called for by a growing people; demanding better facilities of education. But who asks for an academy beyond the pale of civilization, where no roads meet, or church bell is heard; where the crow caws, and the wolf howls?

REMONSTRANCE FROM HIS CHURCH.

When Dr. Wheelock announced his intention to remove his school to some region nearer the Indians, proposals were made to him from various places to induce him to remove thither. Lands, buildings, subscriptions of funds, and sympathy were tendered to him in the spirit of very considerable rivalry. But the most touching appeal came to him from his church, to remain where "Your school has flourished remarkably, grown apace. From small beginnings, how very considerable it has become—evidence that the soil and climate suit the institution. If you transplant it, you run the risk of stinting its growth, perhaps of destroying its life, or, at least, of changing its nature and missing the pious aim you have all along had in view," as the letter from the church to him of the date of June 29, 1767, pathetically sets forth. The letter further says,—"This is its birthplace; here it was kindly received and nourished, when no other door was set open for it; here it found friends when almost friendless—yea, when despised and contemned abroad.

If you remove the school from us, you at the same time take away our minister, the light of our eyes and the joy of our hearts, under whose ministrations we have sat with great delight. Must, then, our dear and worthy pastor and his pious institution go from us together? Alas! shall we be deprived of both in one day? We are confident you will not be displeased at our addressing you, but that you would rather think it strange if we should altogether hold our peace, when we understand it is still in doubt, both with yourself and friends, where to fix your school, whether at Albany, or more remote among the Indian tribes," &c.

SELECTION OF LOCATION.

It would seem, from the date of this letter, that Dr. Wheelock must have filled up two or three years in maturing his plans of removal, and in the selection of his future location. Undoubtedly many places were carefully examined by him, letters written, overtures made, and probabilities of success laboriously scrutinized. He at length accepted the terms arranged by Gov. John Wentworth and probably by Gov. Benning Wentworth, resolved to remove to Hanover, and prepared his charter. Future research for the correspondence of the time among the parties will perhaps develop other reasons for his choice of Hanover. Vermont was not in a condition to give a charter. Massachusetts and Connecticut had colleges, and would naturally enough at that time object to another. Gov. John Wentworth, after a standing refusal of Gov. Benning Wentworth for a dozen years to give a charter to the clergymen of the eastern part of the state, found his opportunity, not only to encourage the great zeal of Dr. Wheelock in his Indian conversion, but to rid himself of the plan of his ministerial neighbors, which undoubtedly favored independency too much to secure his confidence. It might seem quite remarkable that Gov. Benning Wentworth should have refused a charter to the clergymen of eastern New Hampshire, and yet give five hundred acres of land in Hanover to Dr. Wheelock and his Connecticut clergymen when Gov. John Wentworth had concluded to give him a charter. But the old feeling between the

English church and the Puritans was especially rife in New Hampshire, the royal governors and official men in Portsmouth being anxions to head off the prevalence of Congregationalism and establish Episcopacy in the colony. The charters had reserved the best pines for the King's masts, and also lands for the church—a kind of seal of subjection to King and Bishop.

HOW THE CHARTER WAS OBTAINED.

A very singular fact is stated by the late Dr. Allen, who was President of the University, and son-in-law of the second President Wheelock, touching the granting of the charter of the college. Dr. Allen had possession of the Wheelock letters and papers, and many of the papers belonging to the college archives proper. In his "Memoir of Rev. Eleazer Wheelock, D. D.," found in the August number of the *American Quarterly Register* for 1837, he says,—"Among these papers is an original copy of the charter, which Dr. Wheelock caused to be prepared and presented to Gov. Wentworth. In this the title is 'Dartmouth Academy,' instead of 'Dartmouth College.' The words are,—'We appoint our trusty and well-beloved Eleazer Wheelock, Doctor in Divinity, the founder of the said school' (meaning Moor's Indian Charity School), 'to be president of the said *Academy.*' In the charter the words are the same, except the substitution of the word *college* for both *school* and *academy*, and this probably by mistake of the transcriber."

This change of name must have been rather by order of the governor, that there might not in the future be any doubt as to the prerogatives of the institution in establishing professorships and conferring degrees. Dr. Wheelock had called his institution a *school:* the *school* was still to exist; and he now wished to add to it another institution which could, without question, confer degrees, as he was thereafter to educate men for the ministry, as well as Indians for teachers. Academies were not known; and although the term was well defined in Greek and Roman history, but quite different in character from his proposed seminary, yet the name would be honorable, and with the powers of a college would be likely to challenge less hostility and remark if he did not take the name of college, as if equal to Harvard and Yale. The clergymen in the eastern part of New Hampshire had asked for an academy or college, and been refused. He perhaps thought best to ask only for an academy; but when the governor came seriously to the work of giving a charter for a literary institution to the people of his beloved state, he changed the charter to meet his views of an institution. "He struck out one or two clauses," says Dr. Allen, "and omitted some of the names of trustees mentioned in the charter, even the Bishop of London, whose name had been agreed upon, and inserted names of civil officers without agreement."

Dr. Allen says,—"It appears further, from the negotiation with the governor, that Dr. Wheelock proposed to remove his school to New Hampshire, on condition of obtaining an act of incorporation of Dartmouth *academy*, and satisfactory grants of land; and that Gov. Wentworth gave a charter of Dartmouth *college*, with a liberal endowment from the government and from individuals." "The long preamble to the charter," says Dr. Allen, "is to be considered only as a history of Moor's Charity School, and of the circumstances which led Dr. Wheelock to apply for a charter of the college, and not proving at all that the school was merged in the college." The power of the college trustees over the school was at once called in question by the English and Scotch friends of the school, as the school had been committed to certain London trustees, who had no recognition in the charter. Dr. Wheelock announced to them that the school remained as before, without legal connection with the college; that he was president of both, and could resign one and hold the other. The two institutions were managed, financially, with a slight mixture of confusion, but essentially under the president and trustees of the college, till 1807, when an act of incorporation was obtained for the "school," and the trustees of the college forever after were to be trustees of the "school;" but the funds of the "school" were to be kept distinct, and applied according to the designated uses of the donors.

PETITION OF CLERGYMEN IN EASTERN NEW HAMPSHIRE.

In 1758, the Congregational ministers of the Province of New Hampshire, at their annual convention at the house of Rev. Mr. Pike, in Somersworth, "taking into consideration the great advantages which may arise to both church and state from the erecting an academy or college in this province," unanimously voted " to petition the governor for a charter," and appointed eight of their number to wait on the governor and present their petition, then prepared and signed by Joseph Adams, moderator. At the meeting of the convention the following year, at the house of Rev. Mr. Adams in Newington, the committee reported, verbally, " their proceedings and conversations with the governor upon said affair, by which, notwithstanding the governor manifests some unwillingness at present to grant a charter agreeable to the convention, yet there remains some hope that, after maturer consideration and advice of council, His Excellency will grant such a charter as will be agreeable to us and our people." Thereupon, the same committee, consisting of Rev. Messrs. Adams, Pike, Cotton, Parsons, Gookin, Langdon, and Haven, were charged " to do everything which to them shall appear necessary in the aforesaid affair in behalf of the convention, and, moreover, to consult upon any other measures for promoting the education of youth, and advancing good literature in the province," &c.

Messrs. Farmer and Moore, compilers of the first volume of " Collections, Topographical," &c., " relating principally to New Hampshire," say, that " In 1762, the plan of the venerable Dr. Eleazer Wheelock was made known to the convention, and received their hearty concurrence. The foundation of Dartmouth college was soon after laid by the persevering exertion of Wheelock and his friends." They also say that " a spirit of jealousy seems to have existed against their plan [the convention plan], and though they frequently urged the utility and necessity of a college upon the officers of the government, no charter could be obtained until that granted Wheelock in 1769." In " Annals of Portsmouth," Adams says,— " Gov. B. Wentworth would have granted the charter, if the college could have been put under the direction of the Bishop of London."*

DR. WHEELOCK SUCCESSFUL.

Dr. Wheelock must have made annual visits, to obtain funds, to the good men in New Hampshire, and must have pressed his Indian enterprise upon the governors and clergymen of the state. The ministers were urging the governor for a charter; but for reasons apparent or concealed, the governor withheld his grant *from them*, and gave it *to him*. How this result was brought about, and why a college for New Hampshire should have been granted by a New Hampshire governor to Connecticut management, is, at this remote day, somewhat of a problem. The clergymen of eastern New Hampshire had urged their claim on the governor for a dozen years. They were the early ministers, had built up their churches, and cherished the interests of learning; they saw that the state must build up for herself, as Massachusetts had done early and Connecticut later, institutions of learning, and must keep pace with the growing sentiment that freedom must find foundation and support in the education of the people. They urged in their petition " the great advantages of learning, and the difficulties which attend the education of youth in this province, by reason of our distance from any of the seats of learning." They probably hoped to locate the institution in Exeter or Concord; at any rate, not in the woods, where there were neither people

---

* The plan of Dr. Wheelock, laid before the convention, was undoubtedly the same indorsed and recommended the same year by twenty-five ministers of Connecticut, and related wholly to his "Indian School" and efforts for their civilization, for we find three years afterwards, in 1765, he obtained the approbation of his "Indian Charity School" and of his labors from six governors of different states, five judges of state courts, twelve men holding high civil office, clergymen of different states, merchants, lawyers, and doctors—in all, seventy. The document bears date New Jersey. His school embraced some twenty scholars, about half being Indians, and in 1765 two were approved as missionaries, and nine Indians as schoolmasters, by a commission appointed for the purpose. We get a glimpse of the Doctor's restless diligence to make his school a success by the recommendations thus given, and also by entries of donors' names in his "Narrative of Moor's Indian Charity School." His donors were found among the rich men of the country all along the coast, and obtained only by personal appeal and influence. Frontiersmen would give him little sympathy and less aid, having more *fear* than *love* of the Indian. Benevolence seemed to them in conflict with their protection. It was a trial of their Puritan faith to be kind and sympathetic towards those who had cruelly resisted their progress for a hundred years, and who still gave the remote settler great anxiety for his safety.

nor roads, and not to have any voice in its board of direction. The "jealousy" spoken of was undoubtedly sharp and decisive, for in the charter, when granted, not one of those New Hampshire clergymen was given a place in the board of trustees, nor did one ever find a place in the board.

HANOVER SELECTED. N. H. GRANTS.

After two or three years spent in conference and inquiry, Dr. Wheelock selected Hanover, obtained his charter, and prepared for the removal of his family. Hanover, bordering on Connecticut river, was one of the towns, which became involved in the controversy relating to the "New Hampshire Grants." The first Governor Wentworth granted one hundred and thirty-six towns west of the Connecticut river, towards the Hudson, under his construction of his commission, in what is now Vermont. Fifteen other towns on the east side of the river, and beyond the line of the Mason grant, in the centre of which was Hanover, were also complicated in the sad quarrel about the "New Hampshire Grants," technically so called. New York[*] claimed some part of the same territory, as did also Massachusetts, and the settlers were annoyed and harassed by the conflicting titles and jurisdiction of the three states. These disaffected towns were in a state of turmoil and conflict for fifteen years before Vermont was quieted in her present boundaries, and more than twenty before the state was admitted to the Union.

Some important interests of the college were involved in this controversy, obliging the Faculty to mingle in the deliberations and proceedings of the day. Connecticut people had settled the towns on both sides of the river, and, under the vexations of disputed titles, naturally enough sympathized, *en masse*, in the combinations formed to protect their interests and advance their convenience. Hanover was well situated to become the central figure, the rallying-point and power, in the struggle. Here was the college, and men of influence and learning.

---

[*] The Earl of Dunmore, while governor of New York, granted land in Vermont to the amount of 511,900 acres, all of which had been previously granted by Gov. Benning Wentworth of New Hampshire.—*Vermont Records*, vol. 2, p. 94, note.

Young men from all the country around gathered here for education, and their friends were expected to support the institution, and build up the character and material interests of the place.

The president's parish in Lebanon was known as "Lebanon Crank." Parishes were then *quasi* corporations. Governor Wentworth had given the college 500 acres of land, and the state had given Dr. Wheelock, by statute, special jurisdiction over three miles square. This territory received the name of *Dresden.** In subsequent proceedings, Dresden was often considered a town, but Hanover and the state ignored her corporate existence as well as name.

Most of the public demonstrations for forming a new state out of the Grants occurred towards the close of the life of the first president, but they showed quite conclusively that the faculty of the college were participants in various plans to make Hanover a central point.† While Vermont maintained a sort of jurisdiction, the people of the Grants were restless, provoked, rebellious, sometimes asking aid of the states, and sometimes threatening to join Canada in loyalty to the King. At one time a state was projected by union of the Grants on the Vermont side and thirty-five towns on the New Hampshire side, to be called New Connecticut; at another, the sixteen river towns asked to be received by Vermont into their state, and notified New Hampshire they had left New Hampshire; and still another, sixteen towns on the east side and as many on the west side of the river made an effort to form a state; and once the whole Grants of the west side of the river wished to be joined to New Hampshire.‡ In most of the schemes for a new state Prof. Woodward was a prominent participator, with other *Dresden* gentlemen, in contemplation of making DRESDEN a

---

* Belknap says,—"The name of Dresden was given to the district belonging to Dartmouth college," and the petition of the president to the legislature of New Hampshire was, " to have three miles square set off from Hanover and Lebanon as a distinct parish, to be under the immediate jurisdiction of Dartmouth college, agreeable to a promise in writing, under the hands of the Board of Trustees." *N. H. Prov. Papers*, vol. 7, p. 280.

† *Belknap, New Hamp.*, vol. 2, p. 341-343.

‡ Vermont conducted its military operations during the war independent of the United States, raised and paid its own troops, emitted and redeemed bills of credit, and paid its own debts. *Noah Webster's Am. Selection*, 3d part 121, ed. 1793.

STATE CAPITAL. It was said the people had a right, after the declaration of independence, to form themselves in such new communities as they pleased; that rejecting allegiance to the King left them *nowhere*, and they might as well claim local freedom, and escape the tyranny of New York, Massachusetts, and New Hampshire.

These disturbances gave opportunity to a few leading patriots in the Grants to cheat the Governor of Canada and the Captain-General of the British forces there into an alliance of protection, or rather of suspension of warfare, on the Grants during the war. The Haldimand correspondence and other papers, lately published in Vermont, prove that during negotiations for exchange of prisoners on the Canada lines, suggestions and intimations sprang up between our commissioners and the British commander, that the Grants, enraged at their oppressions, would prefer to remain loyal to the King, and so escape the desolations of the war. The negotiations did not embrace more than half a dozen Vermonters, who kept Washington informed of the movement, and thus the Grants and the college were spared the tramp of the army, and the devastations of invading forces which remained in Canada.

Mr. Walton, compiler of the "Records of Governor and Council of Vermont," vol. 1, p. 278, says,—"There are other circumstances which indicate that the officers of the college corporation were very active in the projected union, if not the originators of it. The first convention was in Hanover, and its committee asked for the union. Vermont assented, admitting the identical Dresden, which the president wished should be an independent town, but which New Hampshire had rejected as a town, adopting the college and especially honoring Bazaleel Woodward, who was a professor in the college;"* and in "A public defence of the right of the New Hampshire Grants (so called), on both sides of Connecticut river, to

---

* "He seems to have been active from the first in promoting the union of the western New Hampshire towns with Vermont. He represented Dresden (the college lands in Hanover) on the first union in 1778, and again on the second in 1781. During the second union he was appointed judge of probate of the district of Dresden, one of the agents to congress, and a judge of the superior court. His official service in Vermont of course terminated on the dissolution of the eastern and western unions in 1782." *Note of Walton, Vermont Papers,* vol. 2, p. 144.

associate together and form themselves into an INDEPENDENT STATE," printed at Dresden, 1779, it is said,—" In the early settlement of this country, the Rev. Dr. Wheelock's charity-school, founded on the most noble and benevolent basis, and incorporated with a university by grant or patent from the King of Great Britain, was introduced and settled in this part of the country,—which we esteem an inestimable benefit and advantage to this new state, as well as to the continent, and which the inhabitants of this state are disposed to patronize to the utmost; but, on the contrary, if it falls into the state of New Hampshire, it will be in a state which has heretofore (as such) shown a very cool disposition towards it, and probably will continue the same neglect of it, and principally (perhaps) on account of its situation."* Some future historian will fill a bright page with this wonderful denouement and cousequent great salvation of the people of the Grants and preservation of the college, which would have attracted the spite of the enemy.† Dr. Wheelock's letters to Gov. Trumbull and to Washington, upon the position of the Indians in the pending strife, give no uncertain sound as to his loyalty to freedom. He gave up his scholars for soldiers, and his son as lieutenant colonel, under Col. Bedel of the continental army.

Governor Benning Wentworth, perhaps under the charter enjoining the promotion of religion and learning, in making grants of townships of His Majesty's lands, reserved or gave one share of the seventy, into which his towns were divided, as a glebe for the English church, one for the society in England " for propagating the gospel in foreign parts," and one for the first settled minister, of whatever denomination he might be. He also saved five hundred acres for himself. This Hanover reservation was given to the college, we conclude. Whether Gov. Wentworth was the only governor in the country who was so thoughtful and liberal, I am not at this moment

---

* Pamphlet, page 51.

† "While the war continued, however, these negotiations with the enemy were carried on with much address, and so successfully as to prevent any further hostilities from Canada. A correspondence was kept up which was known only to a few persons, and chiefly managed by Ethan Allen and his brother Ira Allen. While this could be done, Vermont was safe from attack." *Vermont Papers,* 2d vol., p. 485.

able to say. One hundred and twenty-five such townships were chartered in Vermont and many of the earliest towns in New Hampshire, with the addition of one share for the benefit of schools. As very few Episcopalians were found in Vermont, the shares given them, as well as those for the English society, remained unsought and waste. It was proposed to have the legislature sequester them for the use of Dartmouth college, for the purpose of promoting education in Vermont by advancing the interests of the college. "Certain advantages were to be enjoyed by Vermonters at that institution and at certain proposed academies." The proposition failed, but parties sprang up all over the state to obtain the lands, and lawsuits continued down to 1840 about them.

REMOVAL. HARDSHIPS AND PROGRESS.

Dr. Wheelock, having settled the great question of the location of his future labors, without any great amount of preparation for removal, plunged into the wilderness, not knowing what might befall him there. The miles were very long in those days, and there were a hundred and fifty of them to the grant of Governor Wentworth for his college; and the roads were rough, and some of the rivers were without bridges. There was not a house within four miles of those great pine trees, standing two hundred and fifty feet above the soil, and not a tree of the five hundred acres had been cut down. Lebanon, four miles below, had about two hundred inhabitants, and there were some twenty families four miles back in the town of Hanover. Now, look for a moment at the heroism and courage, the Christian faith, and desperation, too, of our first president. He had gathered large funds for his school. The donors were looking to him for results he had encouraged them to expect; he saw his expectations were to fail in Lebanon, Conn., and uncharitable judgment would be indulged in by his patrons, of his efforts, as well as of his wisdom. He saw, too, that his wilderness enterprise involved various disasters, and perhaps utter overthrow of his new movement. A long storm or flood during their journey,—a fire might start in their new village, or in the forest around them, and destroy their homes and substance,—winter snows and frosts, or summer miasmas, might more than decimate his family and people, as the Pilgrims were stricken at their first landing,—or he, like Moses of old, might die in view of the promised land, not being spared to do what no one else would think could be done. But he trusted in the arm of the Almighty, and braved every danger, that the great undertaking of his life might not fail, or confidence in his judgment be impaired. His family, his servants, his laborers and scholars, numbering seventy, with cattle and carts, furniture and clothing, with books and implements of husbandry and the arts, make their way wearily and slowly, in 1770, to the spot where now the college buildings stand. Trees were felled and made into log houses,—some half a dozen,—with one large enough for the college dormitories and a recitation-room. Grounds were cleared; roads were built; Mink brook was made to run a corn and sawmill; chapel exercises were conducted at times in the open air, classes formed and instructed, and the first commencement made to come off in 1771, and a Master's degree conferred upon four young men.

Dr. Wheelock had seen sixty winters, but never such an one as he endured in that of 1770–71. The storms and snows and cold came direct from the north pole. Snow-shoes and buskins, mittens and hand-sleds, were often the only locomotive means of access to the outside world, and supplies must come from the nearest log-house farmers, or, when teams could conquer snows five feet deep, from river towns far down toward the sea. But there was wood enough, and fires enough, and pine knots enough, and enough " bean porridge hot and bean porridge cold," to keep the school and college up to studies, to their recitations and their lectures.

Dr. Wheelock was intensely busy; his bow was never unbent. He was president of the college and preceptor of the school; his eye located the site of the future college building, laid out the present beautiful park around which the officers of the college and men of business should dwell. He located the roads, superintended the clearing of the lands and the building of the bridges and mills. Hear what he says of his family and operations his third year: " For six months in the year I have thirty to forty laborers, beside men in the mills, kitchen, wash-house, &c.; the last year about eighty students, dependent and independent, beside my family, consequently large. I have seven yoke of oxen, twenty cows; have cleared and fenced fifteen acres of wheat, and have twenty acres of corn; have cleared pasturing, sowed hay-seed, and girdled all the growth on five hundred acres. I have enclosed with a fence about two thousand acres of this wilderness, to restrain my cattle and horses. A little more than three years ago there was nothing here but a horrible wilderness; now eleven comfortable dwelling-houses, beside the students' house, barns, malt- and brew-house, shops, &c. I live in my little store-house;—my family is much straitened, but cannot afford to build for myself."

All these operations were in the name of the college and the property of the college; he received no salary,—only his support. Upon his request, the governor appointed a person to audit his accounts. He acted as treasurer, and we hear little of the trustees. In his accounts for 1770, £742 were expended "for labor, provisions, materials," &c. In 1771, for the same, £859; for 1772, £515, and 1773, £1447. At the commencement this year, there were six graduates and nineteen honorary degrees. A three-year-old college in the woods conferring *honorary* degrees! Only think of it!

INDIAN CONVERSION A FAILURE.

Well, the Doctor had established his college and was giving degrees to the pious young men who were to become missionaries to the Indians; but how stood the great question of the conversion of the Indian he had so long labored to accomplish? Alas! alas! The Indian would not come to his school, or stay converted after he returned to his tribe. "My rising hopes," he says, in 1772, " respecting individuals, have heretofore been so sadly disappointed, and I have seen so much of Indian ingratitude, hypocrisy and deceit, enmity and malevolence, to their best friends and kindest benefactors, I should be quite discouraged, but for other considerations which press upon me to bear down all discouragements." He, however, kept out his missionaries at an expense of £150 in 1772, and maintained in his school all the pupils his missionaries could send him ;—but the difficulties were radical. There were convictions of great injustice, embers of old hostilities which the Indian heart could not forgive ; and confidence, to any working amount, could not be obtained. The Revolutionary war soon came, and the Indians very naturally took up the fight against us ;—so *hope*, as well as the *Indian*, failed. The record is, that thirteen persons, missionaries, school-masters, and students, were supported more than half a century from the funds of the school.

There was an element of power and success in this great work to which I should allude. From whence did he expect to get his scholars for his college? The Indian might not come, and the log-house boys were poor. But Dr. Wheelock was a Connecticut man, educated at Yale, and had attained the very highest rank among the very learned divines of his state. He was a most eloquent preacher, and an accomplished teacher. His school had given him wide-spread reputation, and the novelty of his enterprise attracted great attention. The young men of Connecticut were, therefore, drawn to him, and also the sons of the early settlers in towns on both sides of the river up to the college, those towns having been settled mostly by Connecticut people, and incorporated by names of towns in Connecticut. During the first ten years, forty-two young men from Connecticut received degrees out of one hundred conferred during that period, Massachusetts thirty-five, and New Hampshire twelve, leaving twelve for Vermont and other states. The long and deep stretch of wilderness, northwest of Concord and Plymouth, prevented the young men of New Hampshire from a resort to Dartmouth.

Another element of success was found in the religious features of the education, and very small expenses of living at the college. Money was high and food was low ; corn was worth three shillings per bushel, and beef three to four cents a pound. Dr. Wheelock paid his men three to four shillings a day, and servant girls in their checkered aprons received as many shillings a week. He charged in his accounts five shillings per week for board, lodging, and washing for Indian scholars.

DAILY LABORS AND DUTIES.

Dr. Wheelock, in his "Narrative for 1773," under date of October 15, says,—"To give a more clear view and conception of my situation, exercises, and labors in this new world, I shall give an account of *this day*, not because there is anything special, more than has been common to every day, but because I know now what is actually before me.

"Three men are employed in clearing land at Landaff, to prevent the forfeiture of that town; one man is supposed to be now returning with stores from Norwich, in Conn., two hundred miles distant, with a team of six oxen, with whom I expect one or two teams more, which are to be procured there; three laborers at the mills, repairing some breaches, and fitting for use; fourteen employed about my house to prepare for my removal there; two employed in the college kitchen; three digging cellar for the new college; five gathering in the Indian harvest; four receiving and counting brick which I bought at Lyme; several at Plainfield, digging and preparing limestone to be burnt for a *tryal*, whether a supply can be got there for the new college,—all necessary, and neither can be with prudence omitted."

On the same day, and daily, he attended chapel services, instructed a class, and directed the studies and counselled three tutors of the college, as he could not maintain professors; also, looked after Moor's school, under college students. He was the magistrate of the whole neighborhood, but evidently had little business in this line, as he says he " is blessed with a peaceable family, diligent and orderly students, and faithful laborers. I have not heard a profane word spoken by one of my number, nor have I reason to think there has been one for three years past, nor do profane persons expect to be employed in my service, or allowed to continue here. I have found nothing more necessary to maintain good order and regularity than to show what is the law and mind of Christ, what will please God and what will not." "My government is parental." He says,—"A number of students have done much to lessen their expenses the last year by turning a necessary diversion to agreeable manual labor, and many will probably do so for years to come."

CHARACTER OF THE STUDENTS.

The whole country remote from the seaboard was filled with the log-houses of the first settlers. Some of them were still standing in my young years; and even the honored Rev. Dr. Bacon, of New Haven, who is a Connecticut man, and still living, says his "early life was nurtured in a log house, where the wolf was a neighbor, and penury no stranger." Many, perhaps most of the students of Dr. Wheelock left log houses to come to the log houses at Hanover, if not by natural attraction, certainly without aristocratic aversion, and readily ran along in the groove of low fare, great exposure, and hard work.

EARLY STUDENTS.

We will now call up a few of these young men and *interview* them, and see what they have to say or have said of themselves.

Come, Mr. Ledyard, we have heard a great deal of your sailing with Capt. Cook, and travels to Kamtschatka, Tartary, and Egypt; but please tell us about your year at Dartmouth. Well, he says he was there its *first* year; that he studied the Indians more than anything else; that he was so poor he could not pay his bills, and had become so enamored with Indian life and adventure, that, without a shilling in his pocket, he made a pine log boat, fifty feet in length and three in width, and with a little dried venison, paddled himself down the river,—totally unacquainted with the rapids, rocks, and shoals of that river, less stately now than then, when shrouded by the long line of forest trees, and filled by waters of the wilderness,—to Hartford, one hundred and forty miles. He does not say that his Hanover winter gave him a desire to try the cold of the Arctic circle, or that, having tried it, he sought the extreme heat of Africa to find the source of the Niger. But it is said this venturesome traveller was often benefited in his dangerons wanderings by his knowledge of Indian life and resources. Dartmouth's *first* man was the distinguished traveller

Ledyard, who died in 1789, at the age of 38, in Cairo, Egypt, while waiting the departure of a caravan to Sennaar and the Aga.*

In the class of 1776, we find the name of Abel Curtis, of whom very brief record is made by Dr. Chapman. He is mentioned as having been "born in Lebanon, Conn., and having died in Norwich, Vt., in 1783, aged 28." That " he died a farmer, and was also a judge of a county court." I have one fact concerning him, of interest to the alumni, to which I call your attention, hoping some one who has a taste for the investigation may be stirred to the work. Rev. Mr. Hazen, of Billerica, Mass., placed in my hands the fragment of "A Compend of English Grammar, being an attempt to point out the fundamental principles of the English Language, in a concise and intelligible manner: and to assist in writing and speaking the same with accuracy and correctness. By Abel Curtis. Printed at Dresden (Dartmouth college) by J. P. & A. Spooner, 1779," and measuring six inches by three and a half, while the standard British Grammar, printed in Boston in 1784, for the use of schools, measures seven and one half by four and one half inches, and numbers 281 pages. In his preface, he says,—"There is no treatise extant adapted to the genius and circumstances of the times, and fitted to young and vulgar capacities, which points out the fundamental principles of the English language concisely and intelligibly," &c., and as " there is no prospect that any such performance will appear in print, by advice," &c., " presents his Compend," &c. " The order may be a little *new*," &c. It is dedicated to Prof. Ripley, and he says " it has the approbation of several gentlemen of eminent characters in literature."

I find no mention of this book in the various libraries in Boston, or in Brown's Book of Grammars, and I suppose, like its author, it died early. I wish, however, to raise the inquiry whether Mr. Curtis did not originate the great change

---

* Our own Fessenden, of the class of 1776, in his " Lady's Monitor," thus speaks of him:
" Thus when our Ledyard wandered, faint and weary,
  O'er deserts dismal, desolate, and dreary,
  No kind companion cheered his lonely way:
  Man was as savage as the beasts of prey.
  But woman's care his every want supplied,
  By woman's tenderness his every tear was dried."

in Grammars which soon after followed, reducing the rules and elements of instruction to smaller proportions and greater simplicity, to meet the limited education of those days.

Mr. Caleb Bingham graduated in 1782, and in 1785 he issued his "Young Lady's Accidence,"—a primer of a book of 74 pages, bound in boards, five inches by three, actual measure of the copy I have. He was in college when Curtis's Compend appeared, and graduated one year before the death of Curtis, and three years after the date of the Compend.

I only suggest, further, that Mr. Curtis did not live to protect his bantling; and whoever will read the prefaces of the two little books and examine their contents, can judge of their kinship, and may award to the earlier much of the originality as well as celebrity of the latter. I think Dartmouth is entitled, in this little book of Curtis's, to much of the credit of the new life, simplicity, and brevity thrown into the elementary school-books of the few following years, when American authors drove out of our schools English school-books, "none of which," said Webster in his "Third Part," "is calculated particularly for American schools."

It so happened that Dr. Wheelock took along with him to Hanover a man by the name of Osborn, to take charge of his mills. This man had four brothers, who afterwards graduated at the college—Benjamin in 1775. The mill man, Osborn, wrote to Joseph Vaill, a young man of Litchfield, to come up to Hanover "to obtain a college education, by he'ping him tend the mills;" and Mr. Vaill tells us how he answered the call. He says he "started September 28, 1772, with three others, with packs on their backs, with an axe and one horse, to find their way, as best they might, 180 miles to the college sawmill. We found the mills down in the woods, where the howling of wild beasts and the plaintive notes of the owl added to the gloominess of the night season. We made ourselves bunks and filled them with straw, did our own cooking and washing," and, if you can believe it, they took in a boarder! "The price paid for sawing and sticking boards was one dollar a thousand, and half the toll for grinding. Upon this income we were ourselves to live and offset the board of Sophomore Osborn, one of the brothers, who became our teacher to fit us for college, and whose compensation was cancelled by his boarding with us. We were two years fitting. One of our number died and another returned home, but two others came on and filled their places," so that the mill work, the boarding-house, and Sophomore Osborn's support should not fail. Mr. Vaill entered college, and says he studied in his cold home with pine knots for light, walked four miles a day to his recitations, facing a north-west wind, and often breaking his own path in the new snows. "It is marvellous I did not freeze, as I was thinly clad." "In my junior year," he adds, "my health failing, the president gave me a room in the college, and placed under my oversight and teaching certain Canadian boys, who were to be taught English; and afterwards I had charge of Moor's Charity School, so that I graduated only twenty dollars in debt;" and "I record my gratitude to God for my unshaken resolution to persevere amidst all discouragements." This Benjamin Osborn, teacher of the sawmill boys, became a clergyman of great usefulness, and married the sister of Rev. Dr. Porter, of Andover Theological Seminary; and Mr. Vaill was pastor at the church in Hadlyme, Conn., fifty-eight years, and died in 1850.

Rev. Dr. Dana, one of the presidents of the college, who graduated in 1788, was the fortunate subject of a social arrangement which made an escape for him from all the rough life of the students in his day. Good old Dr. Dana, of Ipswich, Mass., the father of our late president, being at Lebanon, Conn., on a visit to his father, and finding commencement was at hand, took an axe in his carriage and drove up to witness the exercises. Being invited to dine with the Faculty,—for then there were Professors Smith, Ripley, and Woodward,—he remarked he had two sons fitted for college, but he hardly knew how he could sustain them. So a bargain was struck between Dr. Dana and Professors Ripley and Woodward, that the Dana lads should come into their families, and, in return, a daughter of each professor should board an equal time with him at Ipswich,—thus giving the young gentlemen the higher studies of college, and the young misses the more polished teaching and social amenities of more cultivated society. But we may judge of the short commons at both places, by a letter written by the father to his son Daniel, saying,—" He had got together two dollars towards the payment of his bills"!!

Mr. Hidden, of the class of Prof. Adams, 1791, was born in Rowley, Mass. After he had learned the shoemaker's trade, and was about to be married in Gilmanton, N. H., where he had opened shop, being invited to attend commencement in company with his pastor and two or three prominent men of the town, who went out into the wilderness to see Gov. Wentworth's college, he was so delighted with the exercises and the young men, that he postponed his marriage, and fitted for college under his pastor, while working at his bench. He took his tools along with him, and repaired and made shoes till he graduated. After his first year, his biographer says, he, in company with another student, drove on a cow, which greatly diminished expenses; and when he graduated, one friend gave him a guinea for his diploma, another $20 to pay off his bills, and a third friend gave him a graduating suit. (The keeping of cows by students came down to my time.) This man was my childhood's minister;—gathered more than five hundred converts into his church, and planted other churches in other towns around Tamworth, N. H., where he labored from 1792 to 1837. He was true to his lady-love, who waited long for the nuptials, which took place in two months after ordination.

The log-house population of the country was a marked one. Only the bravest and strongest young men and women dared to plunge into distant townships, with an ox team of furniture, food, and rough implements of farming, to drive back the wild beasts, and convert the forest hills into productive farms. Hard work and privation were daily duties; but sweet sleep at night gave daily increasing hope and strength. Their children came up with healthful muscle, and minds trained to meet and conquer every difficulty. When these children desired an education, it was only hard work and self-denial in another form which they resolved to meet, as their fathers had met the hard life of the frontiersman. This college, in its externals, was on a level with these young men, and its president was a more eminent man than then filled the chair of either Harvard or Yale, while the same Latin, Greek, Enfield, and rhetoric were studies alike in all. The increase in the number of students, the charactér of the graduates for the first ten years, and their great longevity—nearly half of the first hundred graduates having exceeded the "three score years and ten"—fully establish as well as illustrate the fact, that getting an education under such difficulties was not much of a calamity after all, and that *work*, as Dr. Wheelock taught his scholars, was the best of exercise. If the apothegm is true, "that good men are the stars of the ages in which they live, and illustrate their times," then Dartmouth, during her first half century, may well be proud of her record and her men.

SUPPORT AND FUNDS.

I have little precise information of individual sources of the funds which sustained Dr. Wheelock throughout his connection with the school and college. His "Narratives" show results of collections at periods rather than individual subscriptions. He was said to have had a small patrimony, which he substantially preserved, but which sold for only £1,000 in 1773, when he built his house at Hanover. His salary had been small, and non-payment of it made it shamefully less; but his scholars and school proper undoubtedly brought him in the means of sustaining his low level of current expenses, for he seems to have abhorred debts, and would keep his *outs* and *ins* in pretty even scales. All aid to sustain his school must have been in small sums, as the gift of the small house and two acres of land by Mr. Moor was so wondrous great as to secure forever the name of the giver in connection with the college. The school did but live on its current means, till Whittaker and Occum created a permanent fund abroad.* The Moor gift was the first foundation stone in the whole structure which fills our admiring eyes this day.

---

* Dr. Allen says,—"When his school commenced he sought in every direction, from individuals at home and abroad, and upon the provincial governments, the *charities* required for the support of the Indian youth. The sending of Occum to Europe was a master stroke of policy, although perhaps suggested by Whitefield, who had urged him to go."—*Quar. Reg.*, 1837, p. 29.

The school was now provided for. He had felt of the public pulse, and found a healthful throbbing towards his enterprise, and took courage to enlarge his operations. The new institution soon became, in his judgment, inevitable, both to save him from the past, and to fill up the measure of his great work.

I hardly know how to describe to you the important matter of getting funds for building up and running the school and college by the two Wheelocks, for the sixty years they presided over their interests and prosperity. The dollar was a very large coin in those days, and very few pockets could get many of them, and fewer could hold them any length of time. Few men had had time or opportunity to get rich. The early settlers were clearing lands, building roads, and paying taxes, and how could they give or subscribe to aid in founding a school or college? When a gift of two acres of land and a small house was, comparatively, so generous and large that the donor's name was given to the institution, as the name of Perkins was given to the asylum for the blind in the early history of modern benevolence, the common subscriptions would be laboriously enumerated if they could be found. Moor's gift was in 1753, and gave not only a name but a home to the school. In 1762, it was commended to the benevolent for aid by twenty-five clergymen in Connecticut; and Connecticut, Massachusetts, and New Hampshire legislatures made appropriations. Donations were received, also, from "the London commissioners in Boston," from receipts "in my journey to Boston, mostly from Mr. Parsons's congregation in Newbury;" "from private donations from several quarters, £25." The donations from November, 1763, to November, 1764, amounted to £258; and the expenses of the school and missionaries were not then met, by more than £100. In 1765, the great interest in the school raised his receipts to over £550. Among the donors appear "from a lady in England, £100; from John Phillips of Exeter, £22; from churches in Salem, Rowley, Ipswich, Newbury, Portsmouth, York, Stratham, Exeter, and from various quarters." These moneys were all absorbed in his daily living,—no fund except Moor's.

The indorsement of the Connecticut clergymen in 1762

served his purpose for awhile, but as his views and field widened, he required more impressive recognition and aid. Hence, in 1765, we find Dr. Wheelock obtained an expression of interest in the school from Gen. Gage, commander-in-chief of His Majesty's forces in America; from the royal governors in Massachusetts, New Hampshire, New Jersey, Pennsylvania, Connecticut, and New York; from three chief justices of different states, and large numbers of distinguished men in high official positions, and leading clergymen and civilians from Pennsylvania eastward. Armed with such approbation, and with the results of ten years' successful effort, out of debt, and with three missionaries in distant wigwams, and one interpreter, with eight school-masters at distances from three to five hundred miles, beside eighteen scholars in his school, Indian boys and girls, Rev. Mr. Whittaker and Occum, in 1776, were sent abroad for funds, and returned with seven thousand (7,000) pounds sterling, deposited with a Board of Trust in London, for the school, and between three and four thousand pounds in Scotland, deposited with a Scotch society.

COLLEGE FUNDS.

But now a college was to be provided for. The name "Dartmouth" brought no money to the college. Lord Dartmouth's money was in the school, and the English and Scotch friends looked after the school and were jealous of the college. The Doctor now put his foot into a financial desert, as forbidding as the wilderness he had chosen for his college. Gov. Benning Wentworth gave five hundred acres of land in Hanover, where the college is located, and probably the same reserved to him in the charter of the town. Gov. John Wentworth gave four hundred acres. Other land-owners gave lands to encourage the president to locate there, and the farmers in all that region subscribed labor, materials, and food; some subscribers, however, failed to make good their promises, from alleged inability. Collections of money were made from individuals far and near. John Phillips gave, in 1770, $3,333, and afterwards founded the Phillips Professorship of Theology. A list of names of eminent donors is given by Dr. Belknap, who says the income arising from lands amounted to £140;* and Moore & Farmer said, in 1823, the funds of the college amounted to $50,000, and the income of Moor's school to from $400 to $600 per annum. The state gave £110 for Dr. Wheelock's support, and £500 in 1773 towards the new college building, and afterwards built the Medical college. Gov. Wentworth had built a road, by authority of the legislature, from his country residence in Wolfeborough to the college.

EARLY YEARS OF HARVARD.

We need not feel especially humbled at our early poverty and begging for a living, for Harvard was just as poor in her early days. Rev. John Harvard became the founder by giving half his property, between £700 and £800, and the legislature granted a charter with his name as the first and great donor. " The commissioners of the four united colonies endeavored to stir up all the people in the several colonies to make a yearly contribution toward it, which by some is observed, but by the most very much neglected."† The school at "Newe Towne" became, by acts of the General Court, " Harvard college," at Cambridge, though " the word ' college' was not generally substituted for the word ' school' immediately." This was then a " new world " and a new people, and the institutions of religion and freedom were to " live or die" by " working their own passage," just as every emigrant was doing, by hard work and low fare. The people had, according to the almanac of 1648, " heaps of wheat, pork, bisket, beef, and beer," but after church and school rates were paid, money for a college came hard and slow, even for Harvard.

---

* Dr. Belknap says,—" Among the benefactors of Dartmouth college, the following names are conspicuous : His Majesty George III, King of Great Britain, Earl of Dartmouth, late Countess of Huntington, Prince of Orange, Baron of Hasarswoode, Grand Pensionary of the United Netherlands, Gov. B. Wentworth, Gov. John Wentworth, Paul Wentworth, Esq ; Dr. Rose, John Thornton, Esq., Mr. Forsyth, Dr. Ralph Griffith, of London ; John Adams, Vice-President United States; John Jay, Chief Justice United States ; John Phillips, Exeter."

† *Sibley's Har. Grad.*, vol. 1, p. 10.

THE FIRST PRESIDENT.

Gentlemen, how shall I sum up the character of our wonderful first president? By what imagery, or in what words, can I fix in your minds an adequate expression of his colossal enterprises,—of his executive ability in their accomplishment,—of his indomitable courage and diligence to reach his mark,—of his great love to man and his Saviour,—of the man who, at the close of his life, said he was " almost ashamed to die, he had done so little for his Master"?

The gigantic face of the " Old Man of the Mountain" is seen only from one point, and only then does the observer find the prominences of the adjacent cliffs in such range and combination as to form the features of the great human face,—different features being protuberances of different ledges of rock. Thus the great preacher, the Great Awakening, Moor's Charity School, Dartmouth college, and great zeal for the Redeemer's kingdom, from the start to the end, without a doubt, fear, or rest,—meet in mountain height and projection to form the character of Dr. Wheelock. Those only can comprehend, can compass his greatness, who from one stand-point can take in, in one great whole, the lofty heights to which his amazing powers carried him, in the distinct and herculean labors of his life. His life-size canvas in our picture gallery is expressive of his superiority over the eminent men whose portraits hang upon the walls around him.

I need not tell you he was a scholar. "At his graduation, he was the first Berkeleian scholar," says President Stiles. I need not tell you he was an eloquent preacher. His contemporaries give ample testimony of this; and his revival tours during the Great Awakening place him on the lead, proclaiming to all communities that salvation is by faith, and not by dead forms. I need not repeat how, step by step, and day by day, and year by year, from 1746 to 1762, he obtained funds for the limited expenses of his school by small subscriptions among his Connecticut friends,—or how he enlarged his means, often by applications to legislatures and wealthy citizens from New York to New Hampshire,—or how, by his representatives Whittaker and Occum, spreading the fame of his school, in 1766, in

England and Scotland, he obtained funds and established a board of trust for his school,—or how he plunged into the wilderness in 1770 to meet the Indian half way, and on a higher grade of instruction,—or of the patient, burdensome labor of obtaining funds to support his college till his death, accomplishing so much and yet keeping his expenditures within his means! We stand aghast at such exhibitions of faith, piety, benevolence, such heroism and hard work, and such wondrous power for good hitherto and for ages yet to come. We bless the memory and name of Wheelock, and trust there will yet, though late, spring up, at the bidding of the graduates of Dartmouth, a monument to his memory, in the centre of the common his own eye fashioned, and in front of the college " he went out into the wilderness to see," which shall be alike honorable to his memory and their gratitude.* When the future historian of the college shall give relative force and influence to the great educators of our beloved Zion and country, our first president will stand out in bold relief, as the strong men of the colleges shall come up for grateful acknowledgment. Wondrous man! "Ashamed to die," because thou hadst done so little for thy Master! Thy Master called thee. Heaven only could give thee thy rest and reward. Earth and time will not be ashamed of thee!

THE SECOND PRESIDENT.

But I must speak of Dr. John Wheelock, the second president of the college. Having a brother in the Medical college in 1815, I visited Hanover, and saw the president in his study; and during my fall term in 1816, used to see him; attended his funeral in 1817, and saw him in his grave dress. He was a gentleman of courtly manners, tall and erect, dignified and graceful. I do not wonder his personal friends clung to him in his trials, with lively sympathy and great pertinacity, to his death, or that their memory of him intensified their zeal in favor of the university after. He was a fair scholar and

---

* Dr. Pomroy, of Hebron, Conn., who rode 170 miles to Hanover to preach his funeral sermon, said,—" While Dartmouth, or any of her sons remain alive, while one stone upon another remains of her buildings not thrown down, so long shall the name and fame of Dr. Wheelock be remembered."

careful teacher, and exhibited great judgment in selecting his corps of professors and tutors during his presidency of thirty-six years. Eminent scholars were Professors Smith, Ripley, Hubbard, Shurtleff, Adams, and Moore. Doctors Smith, Perkins, and Mussey were eminent surgeons, and gave life and growth to the Medical college from 1798 to 1838,—men whose praise is in all the land for great professional skill and learning, hallowed by the purest benevolence and social virtues. Ripe teachers made ripe pupils. The great men of the college, down to Choate, were started, stimulated, and fortified by those distinguished men. How the president could keep them, and how they could keep themselves, on the pittance of five to seven hundred dollars a year, is marvellous.

There is very little to say of President John Wheelock. He was son of the first president; had been a tutor of the college, and a colonel in the Revolutionary army in active service. He was called home from the army, on the death of his father, to take charge of the school and college. The charter conferred the power upon the president to appoint his successor, who should be subject to the approval of the trustees. It appears, by the diary of Rev. President Stiles, of Yale college, that though presiding over the college at the commencement in 1779, he had not accepted, but did at a future meeting of the trustees, and was confirmed by the board. President Stiles also says he resigned in 1780, and thereupon the trustees immediately elected him president. He presided over both institutions thirty-six years, obtaining the great merit of sustaining the college upon slender funds, few books, and insignificant philosophical and chemical apparatus.

His corps of teachers, necessarily limited,—funds, beyond tuition, to be begged from house to house as it were,—buildings to be erected, grounds to be beautified, commencements to be made imposing, and the thousand plans of influence and commendation to be formed and pressed in favor of the college,—gave watchfulness and hard work to the president every day of those long years, without leaving any tangible era or especial way-mark for the eulogist to say anything more than "well done." Tall, dignified, and graceful in manner, courteous, affable, and of rare conversational powers, he made strong personal friends, and built up the young college by great zeal and persuasive influence in its behalf. His teachers were eminently successful in making ripe scholars and many distinguished men. Short commons and industrious habits of study, with hard working teachers, laid firm foundations. The second president has glory enough in the Dartmouth catalognes during his official life in saying, " These are my jewels," and, " in them I find my crown of glory."

The second Wheelock lost his presidency by removal. True, perhaps too true. It was not caused by incompetency, nor by neglect of duty or change of religious opinion, but simply to rid the board and college of the family dynasty. The first Wheelock made it a family college. He could hardly do otherwise. The whole enterprise was so burdened with doubt and hard work, that none but members of his family seemed disposed to take tickets in his lottery. The trustees gave little attention to the affairs of the college under the first president. He was sustained in the financial department by English and Scotch funds, and the direction of its physical life lay in the hands of confiding friends and members of his own family. The college and school seemed to him to be his,—creations of his own; and the second president, with power by charter and birthright, naturally enough, thought he and his friends should shape and control its destiny. His long service to build up and sustain the college, moved and influenced by the daily prayer which President Stiles says he used,—"Thou knowest, O Lord, that thy servant has no sinister end, and no other motive than thy glory respecting this school,"—gave religious integrity and zeal to his efforts to maintain his administration over the college. He could not admit impeachment of counsels which had so successfully prevailed for forty years. It was a long and difficult task to supplant individual power, and establish an independent government. The controversy in the church upon the introduction of Prof. Shurtleff was not a matter of religious faith, or hardly of government, but simply to separate the Hanover branch from the Hartford members, who were in the majority. The first president, though a Congregationalist by all his Puritan blood and by the separatist tenacity, allowed

Occum to become a Presbyterian, perhaps for better success abroad, as it certainly proved a power in his success; and though he built his church at Hanover under the name and kind of connection with the Presbyterian church, he was Congregational, and his son, the second president, after him. The internal government was Congregational, by deacons and church meetings of the brethren for business, not elders and sessions; the names were synonymous, but the administration was marked independency. This was a controversy of several years, and developed the danger of permanent family dominion over the institutions.

It was quite natural that the second president should wish to surround the college with the influence and friendships of the family, and that a majority of the board of trust, and even of the faculty, should abide in harmony with the old regime. The father had long been a leader in the great enterprises of his life, and the elements of commander, and even dictator, not offensively so, but in full conviction of right and necessity, had marked his administration; and it was not passing strange that the son, taking the father's mantle by sonship as well as by charter, should claim all its power as well as its position. Overruled by the board and nettled by loss of power, he brought obnoxious charges against the trustees, which led to explanations amounting to recrimination, and thus the breach of confidence and respect became in time so serious that it culminated in his removal by the trustees in 1815. I state the fact. I do not criticize those proceedings. That great honesty of sentiment guided both parties is most clear; but the transfer of personal to public power is sometimes obtained only by successful battle. The president believed in his plans and influence in behalf of the college. But the trustees preferred to give it a more public character and greater independence.*

---

* Any graduate, desirous to trace the line of controversy in the change of the Wheelock dynasty, will find the extended history, running through nearly twenty years, in the "Sketches of the history of Dartmouth college and Moor's Charity School, with a particular account of some remarkable proceedings of the Board of Trustees, from the year 1779 to the year 1815"—a pamphlet of 88 pages; and the answer to it, "A Vindication," &c., published by the trustees the same year—a pamphlet of 104 pages. Both are now very rare. The first is without author or imprint; but the introduction states,—"We are indebted to President Wheelock for the facts, and their substance may be relied on as true."

LEGISLATIVE ACTION.

When I entered in 1816, President Brown was in possession of the college buildings, with Professors Shurtleff and Adams, and tutors Henry Bond and William White, both of the class of 1813. In the Medical college were Professors Perkins and Mussey. There were about one hundred and twenty-five students in college. Some of the trustees, the treasurer, Mr. Woodward, and Dr. Perkins, were in sympathy with the late president. The trustees who had voted for his dismissal were in political sympathy with the then Republican party, but the Democratic party was in the ascendancy. Dr. Wheelock and his friends appealed to the legislature for redress. A committee was sent by the legislature to inquire into the matter and report. The trustees met the committee and "frankly exhibited every measure of theirs which had been a subject of complaint, and all the resources of the institution, as far as their knowledge would admit." The matter stirred up great political excitement throughout the state, so that the legislature of 1816, with less discretion than passion, passed acts to amend the charter of Dartmouth college, increasing the number of trustees so as to give a majority friendly to Dr. Wheelock's party, appointing a board of overseers, making teaching by officers not authorized by the new board subject to a large fine, and changing the name to Dartmouth university.

THE TWO INSTITUTIONS.

The university board of trustees met and appointed Rev. William Allen, Dr. Wheelock's son-in-law, president; James Dean and Nathaniel H. Carter were appointed professors. President Allen took possession of the college buildings and library, and Mr. Woodward, treasurer of the college, held its papers and funds for the use of the university. Some ten or twelve students left the college classes and went over to the university. President Brown procured the use of a hall at the west end of the college building, over Stewart's hat store, for a chapel, and kept his faculty and students at their teaching and study as if nothing had happened. The two institutions now moved on quite harmoniously. The scholars remained friendly, and the officers were mutually respectful. Both presidents were remarkable for genial dispositions and courteous manners, noble Christian gentlemen, and were fully impressed with the sharp and serious conflict before them. We all followed the one bell; and for two long years a hundred or more students were crossing the plain, at every ringing of the bell, to their chapel and various recitation-rooms, while a dozen university students were crossing our paths in other directions, giving ample opportunity to crack a joke and chaff each other.

THE LAWSUIT IN N. H. COURTS.

A suit was in due time instituted by the old board against Mr. Woodward, in Grafton county, charging him with the conversion of the funds, seal, and records of the college, at the February term of the court of common pleas, and, by arrangement, it was appealed and continued to the September term at Exeter of the superior court. At this court it was argued by Messrs. Smith, Mason, and Webster for the college, and by Messrs. Sullivan, attorney-general, and Ichabod Bartlett for the university. At the November term, 1817, Chief Justice Richardson gave the opinion of the court against the college. The cause was then taken by writ of error to the February term, 1818, of the supreme court of the United States, at Washington. During the interim between the decision of the state court and final judgment in the supreme court, great excitement existed throughout the state, among professional men and politicians, and various events transpired worthy of recognition and preservation, as skirmishes incident to the great battle.

SEIZURE OF LIBRARY.

The acts of the legislature and confirmation by the state court gave great assurance to the university, but did not especially weaken the confidence of the trustees of the college in the final result. Both parties, therefore, stood on their good behavior at Hanover, but not inclined to waive any admitted or supposed right. The university had gained no legal right under the state court to make further reprisals, nor were the college trustees disposed to surrender any of their possessions. The society libraries became at once a matter of great interest to both parties. The university had possession of the college library (not a very inviting collection for the students at that time), and the students of both institutions were using the society libraries. These libraries were not incorporated, had been instituted and built up by taxes and subscriptions of students during many years, and were now indispensable on the part of the college students. The right of possession or property even, in the college or university, was a matter of doubt, and the right of the majority of acting members over individual members was not even clear. A further difficulty was also involved in the fact that officers and students in both institutions had equal individual rights. The loss of these libraries to the college students would have been disastrous, if not fatal, as the students could not remain without books, and libraries of two thousand volumes each could not be as readily extemporized as the chapel had been.

These libraries were in rooms in the second story, over both front entrance doors of the college building. One evening, while the society of the United Fraternity was in session near the Social's library, Professors Dean and Carter, with a couple of strong workmen of the place, broke down the door of the Social's library. The noise aroused the Fraters, who rushed up to the library just as the party had entered it, having taken along with them sticks of wood which lay in the hall, and soon terrified the assailants into submission and surrender. The professors and men were at once removed to a room near the library (then No. 12), and detained there, until the students, who had been summoned by the bell, had removed all the books of both libraries to private residences on the plain. When this had been accomplished, four students were assigned to each professor and each man to escort them safely home, that we might have evidence of their safe return without molestation from any person, which could be charged to us. I accompanied Prof. Dean to his lodgings in the house of Dr. Perkins, where Prof. Sanborn now resides. We said nothing to him, nor was conversation allowed in the room where they were detained, that we might not be charged with insult or discourtesy beyond the mere detention. When we had put the professor within the door, he turned, raised his hat, and thanked us; we raised our hats also, and bade him good-night. We had a merry hour, afterwards, all over the plain, in shouts and all possible noises, without any interference of the faculty, although the short hours of the morning had arrived.

COURT.—GRAND JURY.—" NO BILL."

Well, we still had possession of the books, and they had failed to secure them; and although *possession* was regarded equal to " nine points in law," some of the students were, in a few days, arrested, and taken before Democratic justices of the peace, and bound over to the grand jury in the sum of $150, for the trespass and false imprisonment of the professors; and the library trespassers in turn were brought before Republican magistrates, who bound them over to the same grand jury in a like sum. Partisan feeling fermented and boiled and spread all over the state; but when the court came, as it did in Haverhill in May, I need only to name the lawyers who attended that term for you to understand why both parties were respectfully heard before the jury, and why, as the court and bar knew the main issue had been taken up to the supreme court, the smaller and incidental questions were considered of little consequence. The grand jury found " no bill" in all the complaints, and we went back to our studies.

DISTINGUISHED MEN AT COURT.

At this term the great lawyers of the state were in attendance,—George Sullivan, attorney-general, Judge Smith, Jeremiah Mason, Ezekiel Webster, Judge Fletcher, Joseph Bell, Josiah Quincy, Parker Noyes, and Moses P. Payson, Britton, Olcott, and Gilbert, men learned in the law, acute in special pleading, and of great power in argument to court and jury;— some of them were and remained peerless in the profession. Mr. Sullivan had argued the case for the university at Exeter, and Mason and Smith for the college. The same court,—

Chief Justice Richardson, with Bell and Woodbury, associate justices,—presided, who had given an opinion in favor of the university. The great question, whether the legislature of the state, sustained by its highest court, would or would not triumph at Washington, was the all-absorbing discussion, and no one wished to mingle with it any local friction incidental to inferior operations like our library questions. Few of us boys had ever been in the high court, and none of us had seen or heard such giants of the law. It was the day when inventors and schemers, as they were sarcastically called, were indulging in visions of hot air pressure and steam power for propelling boats, and all arrangements of high pressure and low pressure, size, shape, and strength of cylinders, which led to more experiments than successes, and to some suits among interested parties. I remember how amused we were, in a logical, scientific, and powerful argument of Mr. Mason, upon one of those issues before the court, during which he sallied off in a torrent of sarcasm upon the pretence of the party that he had made some superior application of steam or hot air, "when," said Mr. Mason, "every old woman in the country had always known of the current of hot air up her kitchen chimney, carrying off all smoke and odor of her cooking; and that her tea-kettle always increased in steam in its nose the more burning chips she had under it." Judge Smith was then under 60; Mr. Mason, 50; Mr. Sullivan, 44, and Mr. Webster, 37. I do not now call to mind a lawyer of that term of the court who has not passed from earth,—Mr. Quincy having just deceased at the age of 90.

STUDENTS VOTING AND TRAINING.

It was found on looking at the statutes that the students who were of age could vote. It had not been claimed. But now there was a strong desire that Hanover should send a representative who would promote the interests of the college as far as it could be done in a legislature largely in favor of the university. A rally was therefore made at the March meeting; and while only a few could claim a ballot, a large number of students went out to the town-meeting to insure protection and fair play. The students were allowed to vote, and quiet reigned at Warsaw. Tit-for-tat, however, was the order of the times, and as soon as the May training came round, we found ourselves enrolled in the militia, and warned "to appear on parade at East Hanover, armed and equipped according to law, at nine of the clock A. M.,"—a measure just as unheard of as the matter of voting. We thought we could get a day's fun out of it, but we had neither guns, knapsacks, nor canteens. Non-appearance would subject us to a penalty. Appearance without equipments would bring upon us various little fines we did not care to bear. We found, however, a provision of military law, that if the soldier was unable to furnish himself with the required equipments, he might apply to the selectmen for a supply; and, if not furnished by them, upon his appearance on parade without them, fines should not be imposed. We all applied for arms, but none came. We appeared at roll-call, and took our assigned place in the ranks at the tail end of the company. But we could not march to their music. We knew our college songs, and could keep time to them; but the *drum* and *fife*, the time and tramp, were too much for us—worse to learn than Greek; as bad as vulgar fractions or Enfield. When the captain, up at the head of the company, cried out "halt," we crowded up all around him to see what he wanted or what he was going to do, disturbing all rank and file, and getting up a general melée. The captain then took a new departure and re-formed his company, placing one old soldier and one student in succession; but this involved individual bickering, and appeals to the captain to settle the question whether a soldier should apologize for stepping on the heel of the student forward of him, to the great hindrance of military improvement by interposing so much complaint and discipline. We had an hour for dinner, and when it was over we began to apply for relief from the afternoon service on account of various illnesses which were alleged, and so persistently insisted on, one after another, and so much time was consumed, that he dismissed his company, and we returned to the Plain with colors flying, having had a tramp of half a dozen miles and a jolly day.

HIGHWAY TAXES.

Our voting joke did not end in our military overture, for we were soon notified to work our tax upon the highway! We found we had twelve hours each, and the highway led from the college towards East Hanover, up the hill where Mr. Balch lately lived. The surveyor was friendly to us; and, having raised a few *hoes* and shovels, out we went in squads of half a dozen, each of us having agreed to work for the other five, reducing our twelve to two hours; and at the end of the two hours, each rendered his account to the surveyor in this form: " I have worked two hours, and have had five others working for me two hours each." So the tax was crossed off, and we returned to our rooms again. We did work well the two hours, however, and all parties seemed satisfied with the idea that a *legal* fraud was not always a *moral* fraud, and that there could be *damnum absque injuria*.

POSSESSION OF THE CHURCH.

As we approached commencement in 1818, great anxiety sprang up about the church in which the public exercises were accustomed to be held. Both parties seemed equally determined to have it. It had been built by the friends of the college, and individuals and citizens on both sides owned pews in it. Legal rights were, therefore, as in case of the libraries, again in doubt. It was understood that men of education and politicians would come to swell the strength of both interests, as indicative of public opinion. There were military men, too, on the Plain, who threatened to bring in the militia, if necessary, to give the church to the university, as having a *prima facie* right, although the college had occupied it as of old. Earlier than usual the people began to pour in, and the town became crowded and intensely excited. Well, to be short about it, students of the college volunteered to take possession of the church the day before, and keep it till the procession should enter. We made no secret of our doings in our mode of defence against any attempt to expel us from it. We carried up stones and placed them in the belfry and at the upper windows, ready to be cast down upon any assailing party, and a man at every lower window with a sufficient cane or club to prevent any scaling party; and thus the night and day were spent, down to the hour of entrance of the procession, and Hanover witnessed two commencements in church and chapel on the same day and hour. Professors Bush, Chamberlain, Upham, Grosvenor, and twenty-four others, took degrees. I cannot now remember how many degrees were conferred in the university, or what their exercises were, except that an eulogy upon the second president, Dr. John Wheelock, was delivered by Hon. S. C. Allen, of Massachusetts.

DECISION AT WASHINGTON.

The autumn term and winter, before the decision at Washington, passed without any special trouble or excitement; officers and students were at their posts of instruction and study,—comparative numbers remaining about the same, and want of funds bringing great anxiety in all directions. The cause had been argued in March, 1818, at Washington, and in February, 1819, the opinion was given by Chief Justice Marshall in favor of the college, only Judge Duval dissenting. Under date of February 2, Mr. Webster wrote President Brown, in his peculiar, sententious style,—"All is safe and certain. The chief justice delivered an opinion this morning, in our favor on all the points. I give you my congratulations on this occasion, and assure you I feel a load removed from my shoulders much heavier than they have been accustomed to bear;"—and to his brother Ezekiel, of the same date,—"It leaves not an inch of ground for the university to stand on." Mr. Hopkinson, the same day, wrote to President Brown,—"The court goes all lengths with us, and, whatever trouble the gentlemen may give us in future, they cannot shake those principles which must and will restore Dartmouth college to its true and original owners. I would have an inscription over the door of your building,—'Founded by Eleazer Wheelock. Re-founded by Daniel Webster.'"

I find, in a letter which I wrote at the time to a friend, and which was returned to me after his death, this description of the scene which followed the arrival of the news at Hanover: "The expressions of joy are excessive. The officers entreated the inhabitants repeatedly to desist, but to no purpose. In Norwich the shoutings were very great, and in most of the towns in the vicinity. The students are much rejoiced in heart at the good fortune, without any public expressions of it."

The correspondence of Mr. Webster with President Brown and Mr. Mason, shows that the decision of the supreme court was certified back to the U. S. circuit court for judgment. In that court, a motion might still be made to introduce new facts, and in the discretion of the court a new trial might be granted. New facts were presented by Mr. Austin, of Boston, to Justice Story, and the motion was by him overruled, and judgment rendered in June, in Portsmouth, for the college.

Notwithstanding this delay in legal proceedings, my letter says the officers of the college had taken possession of the chapel and all the rooms in the college, though the keys had been refused by President Allen, upon demand by President Brown, and that the students had been cautioned not to enter the library, even if the doors were opened, that Mr. Allen might be held responsible for the books. Professors Dean, Carter, and Searle had already disappeared, and it was announced that Dr. Perkins would go to Boston; that six of the students had come back to us, and others had disappeared.

The college had been saved from her judicial perils, and her chartered foundations established; but the terrors of poverty and a wide-spread opposition hovered over her future. Thank God, her perilous night gave way to a morning of hope and a day of increasing beauty and splendor.

MR. WEBSTER'S ARGUMENT.

I must not let this opportunity pass unimproved to revive the extraordinary power and brilliant display of Mr. Webster before the supreme court in Washington. Of the great exhibitions of Mr. Webster's wondrous power,—the Dartmouth college case in Washington, the argument to the jury in the Knapp murder trial in Salem, the speech in the U. S. senate in answer to Hayne, and the Girard will case,—the college effort stands first and most remarkable of all. The subject and the occasion, the interest and the responsibility so personal and absorbing, made full draft upon his great energies. This was in 1818, at Washington, in the great court of the nation, with Chief Justice Marshall at the head of a court,—unrivalled, before or since, in character and dignity,—with the great lawyers of the country in attendance, with men of learning looking on, anxious as to the foundation and fate of the eleemosynary institutions of the country; the room was small, and the *élite* of the city had crowded in. Mr. Webster was to break down the legislation of a state, and the judgment of the highest court of that state, or the college, his *alma mater*, was to be throttled and changed. Well, how did he meet the expectations or fears of the great minds and throbbing hearts assembled there to witness his utterings? I give you, now, the description of Prof. Goodrich, of Yale college, who went to Washington to hear the arguments, and was present. He says (I quote from Brown's Life of Choate):

" Mr. Webster entered upon his argument in the calm tone of easy and dignified conversation. His matter was so completely at his command that he scarcely looked at his brief, but went on for more than four hours with a statement so luminous, and a chain of reasoning so easy to be understood, and yet approaching so nearly to absolute demonstration, that he seemed to carry with him every man of his audience, without the slightest effort or uneasiness on either side. I observed Judge Story sit, pen in hand, as if to take notes. Hour after hour I saw him fixed in the same attitude; but I could not discover that he made a single note. The argument ended. Mr. Webster stood for some moments silent before the court, while every eye was fixed intently upon him. At length, addressing Chief Justice Marshall, he said,—

" '*This, sir, is my case.* It is the case, not merely of that humble institution, it is the case of every college in our land. It is more. It is the case of every eleemosynary institution throughout our country, of all those great charities founded by the piety of our ancestors to alleviate human misery, and scatter blessings along the pathway of human life. It is more. It is, in some sense, the case of every man who has property of which he may be stripped,—for the question is simply this: Shall our state legislature be allowed to take that which is not their own, to turn it from its original use, and apply it to such ends or purposes as they, in their discretion, shall see fit? Sir, you may destroy this little institution: it is weak; it is in your hands! I know it is one of the lesser lights in the literary horizon of our country. You may put it out: but if you do, you must carry through your work! You must extinguish, one after another, all those great lights of science, which, for more than a century, have thrown their radiance over the land! It is, sir, as I have said, a small college, and yet *there are those that love it——*'

"Here the feelings which he had thus far succeeded in keeping down, broke forth. His lips quivered; his firm cheeks trembled with emotion; his eyes were filled with tears; his voice choked, and he seemed struggling to the utmost, simply to gain the mastery over himself which might save him from an unmanly burst of feeling. I will not attempt to give you the few broken words of tenderness in which he went on to speak of his attachment to the college. The whole seemed to be mingled with the recollections of father, mother, brother, and all the privations through which he had made his way into life. Every one saw that it was wholly unpremeditated,—a pressure on his heart which sought relief in words and tears.

"The court-room during these two or three minutes presented an extraordinary spectacle. Chief Justice Marshall, with his tall, gaunt figure bent over as if to catch the slightest whisper, the deep furrows of his cheek expanded with emotion, and eyes suffused with tears; Mr. Justice Washington at his side, with his small and emaciated frame, and countenance more like marble than I ever saw on any other human being, leaning forward with an eager, troubled look; and the remainder of the court at the two extremities, pressing, as it were, toward a single point, while the audience below were wrapping themselves round in closer folds beneath the bench to catch each look, and every movement of the speaker's face. . . . . . . There was not one among the strong-minded men of that assembly who could think it unmanly to weep, when he saw standing before him the man who had made such an argument melted into the tenderness of a child.

"Mr. Webster having recovered his composure, and fixed his keen eye upon the Chief Justice, said, in that deep tone with which he sometimes thrilled the heart of an audience,—

"'Sir, I know not how others may feel (glancing at the opponents of the college before him, some of whom were its graduates), but, for myself, when I see my alma mater surrounded, like Cæsar in the senate house, by those who are reiterating stab upon stab, I would not, for this right hand, have her turn to me and say,—*et tu quoque mi fili!—and thou too, my son!*'

"He sat down: there was a death-like stillness throughout the room for some moments: every one seemed to be slowly recovering himself, and coming gradually back to his ordinary range of thought and feeling."

Mr. Webster was then 36 years of age, about midway of his distinguished life, and midway the life of the college. Mr. Choate graduated the next year, just fifty years from the date of the charter.

PRESIDENT BROWN.

President Brown filled the last five years of the first fifty, and although engrossed in the great lawsuit, he left an indelible mark on the college parchment, equal to the signature of John Hancock to the Declaration of Independence. The treasury was empty, and the controversy was sweeping over the state like a tornado; but *quietly* and *calmly* he took the chair, and, though asked to preside over another college where honor and reward were inviting, his eye and hand were fixed on the one purpose of defending the rights of chartered institutions, for the encouragement of benevolence and learning. His consecration to the defence of the college was entire and untiring; his personal entreaty and influence riveted the friends of the college to both its support and defence. It was said of him, that he so thoroughly informed himself upon the law, the equity, and the vast responsibilities of the question, that he energized the great advocates in the case. He braved the storm and fought the fight. He triumphed;—but worn and exhausted, he fell, in great purity and renown. In the words of another,—" President Brown was commanding in his person, affable in his manners, and exceedingly dignified in his whole bearing. His mind was of a very high order—profound, comprehensive, and discriminating. He presided over the college with great wisdom, dignity, and kindliness, and the students loved and honored him as a father. His whole character,— intellectual, moral, and Christian,—was beautiful." My recollection of him fills a chapter of very loving memories. Such beaming, winning eyes, such affectionate counsels, such earnest religious influence as he impressed upon us, produced in us great love and submission to his wishes. We were all on our good behavior, for our proficiency and bearing were watched by friend and foe of the college. The president had only to intimate his wishes, for us to carry them out. But he was wise and unobtrusive in his communications to the students. Prof. Chamberlain was his unseen private secretary, his confidant and organ, who had also individuals in the different classes through whom any suggestions or plans were quietly promulgated and promoted. Mr. Olcott and Mr. Lang, Dr. Mussey and Dr. Alden, Deacon Dewey and Deacon Long, with the professors Adams and Shurtleff, were supporting pillars to the president in holding the opposition in Hanover in a comfortable state of quiet. President Brown, in his five years, sent out the accomplished scholars Haddock, James Marsh, Fiske, Bush, Prof. Upham, Prof. Chamberlain, Choate, and Geo. P. Marsh, *four* presidents of colleges, and the missionaries Temple and Goodell.

BENEVOLENCE OF A PERIOD.

I have accomplished in these collected historical facts and my own reminiscences, my desire to place before you certain events which are fast fading away, as the actors in them have mostly been starred upon our triennial. They cover only the first fifty years, from the wilderness to Choate; and beyond a few other thoughts, I shall not further ask your attention. During the first thirty years of this century, the Protestant world was awakened to new spiritual, educational, and mechanical life and progress. Missions to the heathen nations, home evangelization, religious newspapers, Sunday-schools, literary clubs and lyceums, were being inaugurated. The press was aroused to new effort and power. Steamboats and railroads, manufactures and the arts, were being established; the ignorant, the poor, the sick, the blind, the insane, the intemperate, the criminal, came up as never before for sympathy and relief. Commerce and agriculture, mineral fields and labor-saving inventions, were creating individual wealth, all tending to and resulting in creating a multitude of benevolent societies, and opening wide the avenues of doing good to others, and of loving one's neighbor in new and ever enlarging ways and processes.

Martin and Mills prayed for the "heathen in their blindness," and the American Board sprung up to send the gospel.

Gallaudet taught the blind to read, and Perkins built an asylum for them. Edwards called attention to the intemperance of the land, and societies were formed for its suppression. Dwight aroused the people for better prisons, Garrison for purer freedom, and Mann for more general education. The religious denominations quickened their energies, in their various ways of enlargement, influence, and support. Love to God and man seemed to be getting the better of mammon, so that dying men gave portions of their accumulations to hospitals, asylums, churches, and schools. " Freely ye have received, freely give," became a living principle. Bartlett poured out his treasures on Andover. The rich men of Boston filled the treasury at Cambridge as often as new wants were made known, and sent their cash drafts back into country towns to establish churches and schools, as their local attachments gave preference. Old colleges were provided with means of enlargement, and new ones established. Such wondrous giving of money for every human benefit or want, as the last fifty years has chronicled all over New England, was never known. And now, the rule and expectation is so general, that, when a man of wealth dies, the first question is, What has he given in charity?

Dartmouth's sons have remembered their *alma mater*, and other persons have favored her, till her buildings are largely increased, her facilities in all departments of learning greatly multiplied and perfected, her days of poverty and short commons forgiven as well as forgotten, with a more learned and successful president, and a larger and more learned corps of teachers than ever before known, and with an ever-increasing honor and power of her graduates.

I am happy thus to have paid my tribute of grateful affection to my college, and to be able thus to bear my testimony to her achievements;—and, in closing, let me adopt the words of Abel Curtis, of the class of 1776, who, in the dedicatory address of his "Compend of English Grammar," in 1779, prayed that " Moor's Charity School might greatly flourish, till the sun and moon shall cease to shine."

ERRATA —On page 43, 10th line from top, and on page 46, 16th line from top, for "Republican" read *Federal*.